# EASY

# TIGER

## EVAN

## NICHOLLS

FUTURE TENSE BOOKS

*Easy Tiger*


Printed in the United States of America
ISBN  979-8-9986256-0-2

Cover + Book Design by Angelo Maneage
Cover Art by Evan Nicholls

EASY

TIGER

# CONTENTS

Discovered in the act,
The man stealing a horse
Mounts and rides away.

—

CHIKAMATSU MONZAEMON 近松門左衛門


I have saved all my ribbons for thee.

—

LEONARD COHEN, 'BIRD ON THE WIRE'

HORSE

THIEF

PHRASE

# EASY TIGER

The tiger makes it all so easy, the way it sweeps the woman's house, packs a satsuma for her snack, accounts for the taxes. The way it ambushes need. How it steps the ache out of her back after work, shifting like a moon man or a dressage horse. This tiger is better people than most, the woman thinks. Still, it is shit at being a tiger. The way it obeys all rules of the IRS.

"WAR LANCE"

# HELL YOU LATER

The man in black came for the dog but the dog said, 'Not right now.'

'Not unless you are a stick,' the dog clarified.

"TRUBLE"

# WHAT A SHOT

Last week we looked up and the moon was a box. Then dad appeared from behind the shed, cradling a slingshot and handsaws. 'I did that,' he said. We said there was no way. He walked off ashamed: 'You would not bat an eye if I was the U.S. government!'

Now the moon has right angles. Now the moon is a wrong peg. Now the moon resembles one of those watermelons from Japan. Every night now the moon begs us to have a little faith.

"DING"

# THE UNWRITTEN RULE OF THE RED HAT CIVILIZATION

Yellow clothes.

# WAR EFFORT

Working at the pillow factory, you fill the sacks with pelican feathers. You also stuff pillows with spoons, lobster meat, carpentry nails, ginkgo leaves. Then you play every pillow like an accordion. You form one after another, stitch them shut with ostrich sinew. The way the pillows slump you find amusing. Perfectly great, how you sleep at night.

# TWO SEATS



*after Rosebud Ben-Oni*

The angel took up two seats on the train. The tuna crossed her fingers. The dart threw a billiard ball at itself. The peacock thought he was a rooster. 'Good god,' said the triceratops, sunbathing in the comet light.

# A LITTLE SONG IN THE TOOTH

The dentist is armed
with a violin bow.
This is how he makes
the patients sing.

# PERCEIVED SLIGHT

That pickpocket nabbed the moon's wallet. That athletic calf was the distraction. That fox saw the whole thing go down. Kept on strangling the chicken. That moon deserved what it got. The way that sonofabitch made light of us.

# BUY THE BUOY

'Buy the buoy,' said the salesman.

'No,' said the person back.

'It would look great around your neck,' the salesman pushed.

The person continued eating their salad.

The salesman resealed his yellow coat.

The salesman returned the wares back to his heart.

The salesman returned to the fetal position and prayed.

For a large fin for a kind man to stroke.

# A REGULAR KNIGHT

He is not a white knight or a black knight.
He is a regular knight.
In regular armor.
With a regular sword.
He does not ride a white horse or a red dragon.
He rides a pony and is accompanied by a large ginger cat.
His armor is actually made of tuna tins.
His sword is actually a little one you find pierced into an olive.
He is not very fearsome.
He is not especially helpful.
He can become very anxious as well.
A regular knight with a regular heart.

"SQUADRON"

# HOLDING COURT

Literally holding a little noble court in my hand. There are small guards with small halberds. There is a beautiful woman in an ugly wig. I have a king throned on my finest nail. There is a bantam executioner. A man with a horn. Far off, a knight warring with an archer on the hill of my thumb. It was agreed upon. 'We are doing this for the good of the country,' the king prays to me at night. I have easy access to a jester, who is planning an assassination. Who secretly believes in the pinky ring.

# WRONG FOOT

Opening the trunk, at midnight in the marsh, you realize you have the wrong foot. You thought you had stowed in there a different bodiless foot, with a bit of mold, handle of bone, with toes that turned to the left save for the pinky toe absquatulating from the rest. A different foot that would have made the perfect squelch in the grass. Instead, your instrument is the foot of a Yamaha piano. You will have to keep your composure to compose. You will have to make due, or you will have to go back.

# TELL ME

Once a week, the warlock cuts off a unicorn head with scissors. He then feeds the head a crisp yellow pear. The heads always talk after, usually repeating a useless bird fact. The warlock's financier, who is supplying the unicorns at great expense to himself, including a double mortgage, thinks the warlock is in the middle of a great spell. He's really just a little freak. As their invariable final act, the heads always grow wings and fly straight into the electric transformer. Why are you freely constructing their nest in your mind? You are not touching the ground.

"SIRE"

# TINY CROSSBOW

You are a knight wielding a tiny crossbow.
You have a job to defend the kingdom.
You carry your tiny crossbow.
Carrying your weapon is no small deed.

"LOST"

"WONDERFUL"

THE

FAMILY

GUN

# SON OF A GUN

The gun was married to a tractor wheel. The tractor wheel's parents were a snowball and a mink coat. The third cousin was a fishing rod. The other in-laws were two moving parts. The niece was a pinball machine. The son said 'This family has no business being together.' Then he split.

# JUMPED THE GUN

The son of a gun robbed his father at knifepoint. When he dug through the wallet, he discovered a picture of himself. These are the situations you find yourself in when you have been raised by a gun.

"F"

# UNDER THE GUN

The tractor wheel was frying donuts for the visit. The great aunt scepter was en route to the house. The gun decided to disassemble the fence. The wife asked why and her eye began to rust.

# SURE AS A GUN

On the street, the gun bumped into a model train. The model train was walking with a drill and a grapefruit spoon. Later, the gun stopped to say hi to a passing colander. The gun was certain the word carried right through her very chest.

# GIVE IT THE GUN

The gun would do spins in front of anyone willing. The gun was that type of gun. When sitting, or eating, or standing, or counting cards, the wife could not help but see herself in the torque.

"HEAVY"

# GUN A BLAZING

The tractor wheel woke up to the smell. The gun had tried making breakfast in the kitchen. The gun could not help but set the table on fire. The next morning he cut his tomato with a fork.

# THE FASTEST GUN

The gun's drawl was so quick it dropped the 'L.' The gun's entire body was his mouth.

"HERE'S WHY"

# STICK TO THE GUN

'Stick 'em up,' the gun said, brandishing sauerkraut at an ice cube tray.

'Maybe you could use these,' the gun said, directing a tee shirt cannon to sticks and stones.

'Stick a fork in me,' the gun said, crying into a chainmail sleeve.

# GUN TO THE HEAD

The gun admitted to cheating last night. The gun told his wife he was feeling overwhelmed. Last night the gun kissed a steering wheel with his forehead.

# GUN DOWN

The gun fell into the lake. The gun fell onto the scaffold. The gun fell for the trombone. It was a meet-cute. The gun fell over. The gun fell like a crutch almost every night.

"GIANT FISH"

"L"

"AN ARMED MAN"

"BEGINNING WITH SNAKES"

"BALLET"

"EAGLE"

"AIRPLANE PLANT"

"ALBATROSS"

"OBLIGATIONS"

"YOR COCK"

"HID"

63

# AMUSEMENT

# TAX

# BACK FROM THE WAR

How your lover
returns

your gaze like
they are taking aim.

How your lover falls
on every step.

How at night, your lover
guzzles the dead

butterflies from a rain boot.

# FATHER CHRISTMAS

Like the government, Father Christmas controls all the weather and the birds. Like your father, he returns in uniform, while you are fastened to sleep.

# SAME SAME

That deer with vampire fangs is holding open the door. Holding it open for you. You are more than a little anxious, but you are already on the move. That deer with vampire fangs looks at you expectantly, like an audit. You know no alternative route. Is it aware you are attending the meeting? Is it the one meeting with you? 'I am running late,' you say upon reaching the entry. 'Same same,' it agrees. 'I am running, too.'

# ARROW ON FIRE IN YOUR HEART

An arrow is on fire in your heart.

Ow.

What a highly unusual injury.

Headless armless legless with an arrow on fire in your heart
and an onion making you cry.

# PARLOR TRICK

The napkin is a wipeable toucan. Your ear is a nibbled coin. All it takes is you, then me. Look— now I grew, from your toenail, an invisible toe.

"MORE"

# MARRIED TO THE JOB

The premise is easy: you are married
to the job. You proposed to the job
and it said Yes. Then the job said
Yes in front of everyone. Now
you roll up your sleeves and make
love to the job. You tell the job
how devoted you are, say you
love it because that is part of it.
Part of marriage. You wake up
early for the job, show just how bad
you care. You are tender and hide
your cheating. Say you want a family.
When you wake, you watch it snore
and you roll up your sleeves.

# SWORN ENEMIES

Today your sworn friend had a good idea. That made you sworn enemies. He said that thing that was so smart, what an asshole. At noon, you will strike each other with twin marsh herons. The birds will be stiff and dead. You will wield them by the yellow legs. The loser will leave forever. You wish you were kidding. Tomorrow you will start your second life. Grow a mustache, wear an aloha shirt. You wish this was a joke.

# HISTORY BUFF

'I have one trillion swords.'

"SUN CONTROL"

# WEST OF VIPERS

Actually, the city of Vipers has a mild population. Yes, some vipers. But there is also a postal worker who skids like a ball. Pelicans who take your trash. This town has a certain 'I don't know what.' Every night, a sarcophagus is wheeled in from the cold. You could be happy in charming Vipers. In the amphitheater, we keep a champion egg. To the west, nothing else is possible.

# EMU KNIGHT

Our emu fell over dead and went to heaven.

Then he miraculously returned to life on earth.

We put him on all the late night talk shows after the fact.

We made him the spokesperson for Orangina.

We knighted him on national radio.

Amazing place this earth, the way it makes you

stay holding onto it with no hands.

# SANS SORENESS SOON

Hit by the popemobile,
you will be sans soreness soon.

# LAIR OF THE DOG THAT BIT YOU

*with thanks to Evan Williams*

You mow the lawn. You vacuum up.

# WOW THE SERVICE HERE

Gale-force winds holding
your hat for you.

# HOT HEAD

We all gathered in the square to burn the pile of confiscated berets.

'Death to the beret!' said the newsboy with a pencil in his ear.

"BARB"

# A SUDDEN SET OF STAIRS

Nobody asked for it, but there it is. In the way of honking cars and bighorn sheep and clementine oranges. People yelling for it to get out of the way, and watch out. The cars are spaced like this: car, car, clementine, car, car, car, clementine. The sheep are traveling between the cars and small fruits and getting into arguments. If you had a car, you would also beep. Everybody wants to go home.

# HEAD CANOE

We take up paddles.
Climb into the mouth.
Sit on the tongue.
Immediately, the head is complaining about water in its ears.
The head is saying its lips are chapped.
We try to ignore it.
We don't know who it once was.
We want to keep it that way.
We want to make it through the rapids.
At the end, pay for a picture.
When we hit the whitewater, the qualms just become worse.
God, we don't look it in the eye.
God, we want to unload.

# LONGEST SAUSAGE

We pull over to look at the world's longest sausage. The sign says it originally started as a roadside attraction. At the world's longest sausage, people are lined up forming the world's longest line. Bearing the sausage on their shoulders. Whenever you are hungry, you take a small bite from a different place. Forget the car, which is now a grassy hill with a bison on the hood. When we step into line, we are naturally ordered. We meet our neighbors. Smile at stray dogs. Sleep standing up.

# WORLD GETTING WORSE

after Angelo Maneage

Nothing especially explains the circumstances.

The blindfold is a blindfold.

There is a large, screaming, severed ear.

There is a worm with a wolf's head.

Are you kidnapped? You are kidnapped.

There is a sad criminal with a plantain to your goat.

You had been minding your own business, eating a halibut donut
on the park bench.

Hey.

Now you're here.

# A THOUSAND TIMES YES

The smallnesses arrived and everywhere we looked, freight ships and tennis rackets the size of thumb tacks. Thumb tacks the size of ions. Those made our feet kill. We even discovered herds of dwarf alpacas, climbing over each other out of bins and taps and marching along handrails. We spun tiny yarns from their fleece. You can only keep so warm with so many diminutive gloves and hats. Yes yes, we said, begging the needles to stop.

"NEED"

THE

FAMILY

GUN

# BEAT THE GUN

The tractor wheel outpaced the gun in a foot race. The tractor wheel wore the victory like a snakeskin boot. 'This never happened,' the gun said, 'back when we were young.'

# HAVE GUN, WILL TRAVEL

Before marrying the tractor wheel, back when he was young, the gun had briefly taken up with a radial spoke somewhere in Arkansas. At night, the tractor wheel wonders what the road is like.

# THE YOUNG GUN

The son of a gun asked his father what he had been like when he was young. The gun said he had been like a rubber chicken or gutter ball.

Really, the young gun had been the bounce of a dinner plate.

"PA"

# CHEKHOV'S GUN

The gun had a bell for a mother. The gun's father was a cheap crate. If the gun's mother ever tried to go off, the crate would eat her with the entire length of his arms.

# GUN FOR SOMEONE

The son of a gun found it difficult to hi-five. The son of a gun could not wrap his head around a gaseous state. The son of a gun did not know how to play catch. The tractor wheel did not know how to play catch.

Although the gun tried. Whenever entering, the gun would hand out his own breath.

# LOVE GUN

The gun gave a letter to his son and it was a baseball. The baseball did not know how to bow.

The gun gave a letter to the tractor wheel. The second baseball read, 'You are my wife.'

"BEG HERE"

# GUN RUN

Tonight, the gun thought of fleeing. Tonight, the tractor wheel envisioned smuggling herself. Tonight, the son wished he could vanish into a bread box.

# GUN SHY

The gun walks into the auditorium with himself on his belt. A known fact: the gun's whole body is his mouth.

"RUPTURES"

# THE FIRED GUN

Did not mean to go off.

# EAT THE GUN

'In the morning, under the right conditions,' the gun whispered to the rest of the theatre, 'I am actually an orange dreamsicle.'

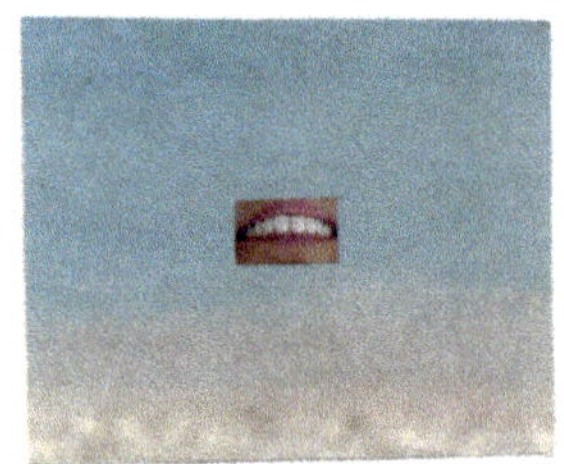

"SMILE"

"BLANKS"

"SPOTTED WITH FLESH COLOR"

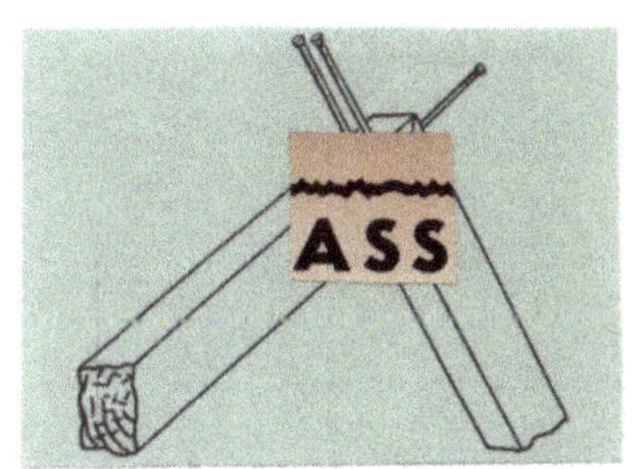


"ASS"

"TIM"

"PLEASED WITH THE RESULTS"

"FANCY BROKE"

"IN STAN"

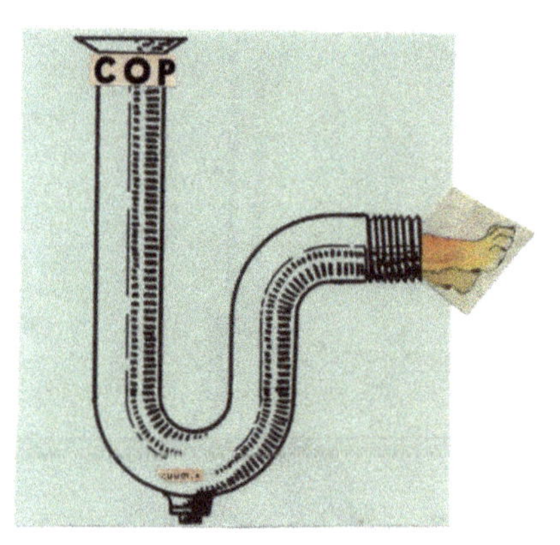

"COP CUUM"

114

"SMEARING HIM WITH FECAL MATTER"

"HOW"

"YOU KNOW"

SOMETHING

MOON

# WHAT HAVE YOU

Fact is the woman gave birth— not to a baby, but to an actual live cat. A mangy cat. We all looked at each other in the delivery room, asking how it came to be. The doctor mumbled about the past, two lovebirds he had found in an x-rayed chest. And before we knew it, we loved the cat. What a great cat. The woman asked about an adoption fee. We said, 'On the house!' How different the light enters up here, ten thousand leagues above the hardness of earth.

"VOLUMES!"

# YOU NAME IT

There is a lump lumped in your throat. There goes the cat with your purple tongue.

You try not to grow so attached, but after all, you do.

# OUR SPLEEN

Our spleen is the size of a dinosaur.

We keep it in the warehouse
and don't really know what it does.

You and I both agree
it's probably essential.

We stand next to the forklift
and look at it.

It's lucky we like each other,
or sharing a spleen would be difficult.

Especially one of this height and weight,
a very gooey, bloody triceratops of dubious origin with a
    mysterious job.

It doesn't matter.
Who cares.

It's not a heart.

In the pitch-black of the warehouse,
you can't even hear our spleen at work.

'Is it working?' you ask me,
sitting around much like a spleen.

Who knows.
I am not a scientist.

It's lucky we have each other.

Otherwise I would be alone
in a dark place with my own large spleen.

You have a forklift.
Our spleen has us.

# ANOTHER YEAR

Tending to a fire at the bottom of the sea.

"WORRIED"

# POPE BOOT

The pope lifted up his robe a little
and showed off his boot.
Then he asked if I would like
to go on a date immediately.
'You and me,' I asked,
'Isn't that a conflict of interest?'
The pope insisted no one would care.
I said I'd rather do it somewhere
more public like a food court.
We were in an airplane.
We were on the last flight out.
Then my nose bled immediately
and he wiped away the blood.
That is how our love story starts.

# DON'T PUT THE TART BEFORE
# THE HORSE

Unless you want to see
a good horse eat his tart.

# YOU CAN LEAD A HORSE TO WATER
# BUT YOU CANNOT MAKE IT SINK

Not even with the swift
blow of a boat oar
or a thick slice
of birthday cake.
Not even the word please.
Not even if it pleases you.
Nothing will make that horse
drown for you
and that is decent.

# MANY HANDS MAKE FLIGHT WORK

It took all day to glue feathers to that horse
and thank god we did.

"FIFI"

"EASY"

133

# KNIGHT IN AN OLD-FASHIONED BOOK

I am actually very apprehensive about getting on the horse.

# EATEN BY A TIGER

I am actually really enjoying getting acquainted on a personal level.

# THE SHARKS SMELL BLOOD

I am actually not the chum I am
the captain's beautiful son.

# MERLIN

I am actually not presently a wizard I am
the fly presently flying into your mouth.

"RIGHT RIGHT RIGHT RIGHT"

# HOLDING THE EGRET

Hold it close to your chest.

You are holding the egret.

There you go.

You are washing the egret.

Wash the egret with a bar of soap.

Feed the egret.

There you go.

You are feeding the egret.

He is good.

Fit this poem into your mouth.

Use this poem like soap.

# LEAVING A SEXY CORPSE

Sorry!

Let me get that out of your way.

# LITTLE INFERNO

Like magic, the magician pulled a fire out of his hat. 'I'm your little inferno,' said the brightest thing on earth.

"GOOD OR BAD"

"POSTHUMOUSLY"

"WELL"

# SCARED TO FALL ASLEEP

## ACKNOWLEDGMENTS

I would like to thank the following people for their contributions big and small to this book, including their guidance and love, direct inspiration, friendship and support: Kevin Sampsell, Emma Alden, Benjamin Niespodziany, Evan Williams, Angelo Maneage, Kiik Araki-Kawaguchi, Gary Barwin, Vik Shirley, Mark Leidner, Zachary Schomburg, Lauren Alleyne, Greg Wrenn, Laurie Kutchins, Kevin Bertolero, Dylan Nicholls, Kat Nicholls, Zach Nicholls, Courtney Conroe, Louis Nicholls, Shawn Wager, Kent Wager, Kyle Wager, Jane Rodriguez, Yosvany Rodriguez, Sue Braswell, Rachel Owens, Brandon Landers, Brenden Rearick, Tea Jofeliz Rinonos, Crow Jonah Norlander, Aaron Burch, Ruby Rorty, David Dodd Lee, Sarah J Sloat and finally Uni the cat.

I would also like to thank all of those involved in the creation, production and distribution of the books, paper ephemera and various media I use for collage. These are primarily vintage materials ranging from the 1940s to 2000s. I especially owe much of my collage practice to my copy of the June 1968 edition of *Dog World*, which has the best fonts, sun-worn paper and pictures of dogs I have ever encountered.

Some of the poems in this book appear in some form at the following publications:

*Cola Literary Review* ("Easy Tiger"); *periodicities* ("Perceived Slight" and "Father Christmas"); *Yalobusha Review* ("What a Shot" and "Back From the War"); *hex literary* ("The Unwritten Rule of the Red Hat Civilization" and "Little Inferno"); *HAD* ("Two Seats," "West of Vipers," "Sans Soreness Soon," "Head Canoe," "Longest Sausage," "A Thousand Times Yes," "Merlin" and "Leaving a Sexy Corpse"); *Mercurius* ("A Little Song in the Tooth," "Tiny Crossbow," "Parlor Trick," "History Buff" and "Wow the Service Here"); *Your Impossible Voice* ("Buy the Buoy" and "A Sudden Set of Stairs"); *Biscuit Hill* ("A Regular Knight," "You Can Lead a Horse to Water But You Cannot Make It Sink" and "Many Hands Make Flight Work"); *Guesthouse* ("Son of a Gun," "Jumped the Gun," "Gun Down," "Sure as a Gun" and "Eat the Gun"); *Rejection Letters* ("Married to the Job"); *New Delta Review* ("Pope Boot"); *Afternoon Visitor* ("Emu Knight" and "World Getting Worse"); *Firmament* ("Tell Me," "What Have You" and "Our Spleen"); *Landfill Journal* ("Knight in an Old-Fashioned Book," "Eaten by a Tiger" and "The Sharks Smell Blood").

**EVAN NICHOLLS** is a poet and collage artist from Virginia. He is the author of two books of poetry and collage, *Easy Tiger* (Future Tense Books, 2025) and *Holy Smokes* (Ghost City Press, 2021). He is also co-author of *There Has Been a Murder* (Ghost City Press, 2022), a poetry micro whodunnit written with Evan Williams and Benjamin Niespodziany. He lives in Charlottesville, Virginia with his cat, Uni. Find more of his work at *enicholls.com*.

www.ingramcontent.com/pod-product-compliance
Lightning Source LLC
Chambersburg PA
CBHW041325120726
48005CB00014B/2133